Baby's
HOME SPACE

Black and White High-Contrast Book

Written and illustrated by

R. M. Smith

CLARENCE-HENRY BOOKS

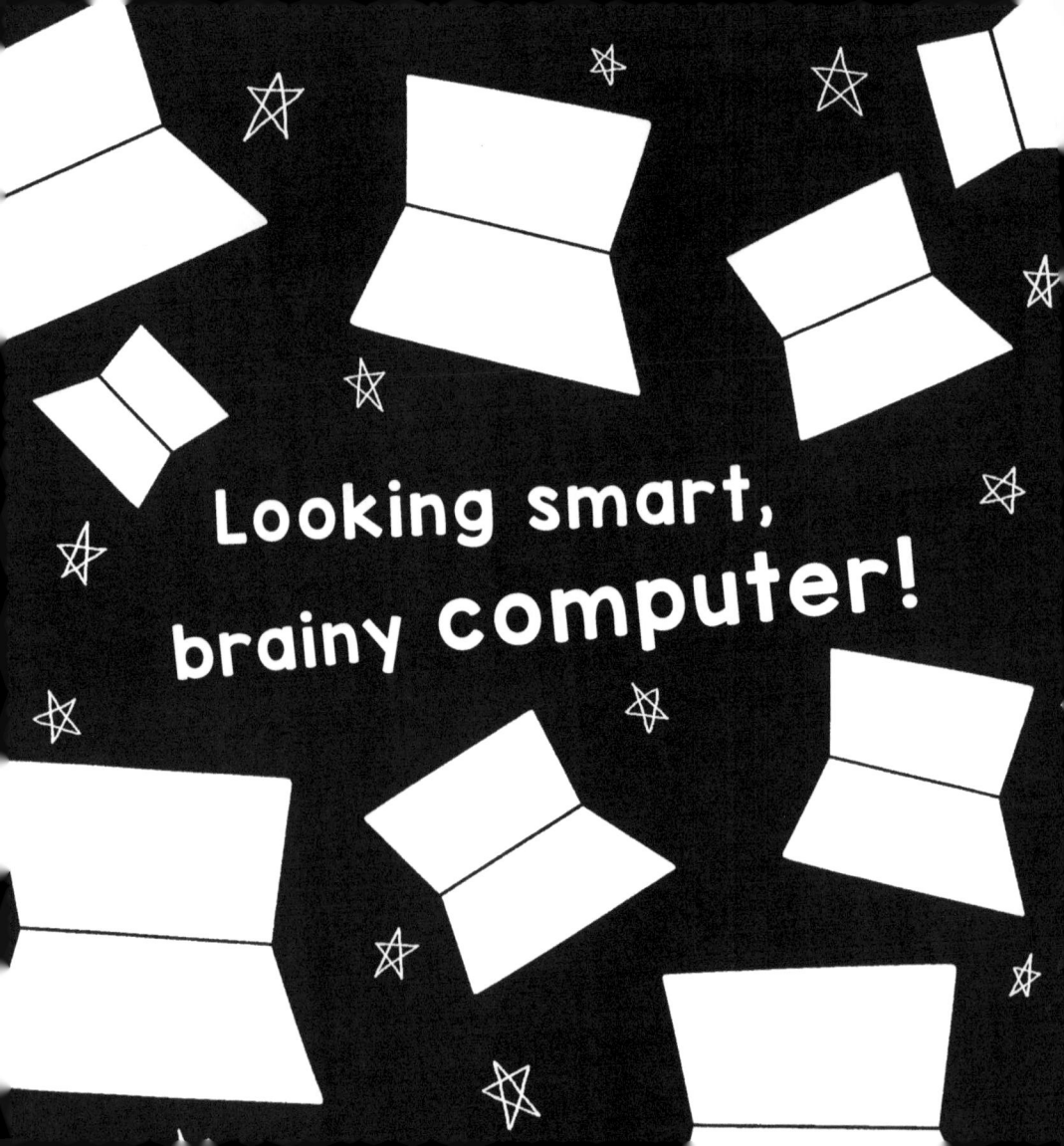

Baby's
HOME SPACE
by R. M. Smith

Clarence-Henry Books • Alexandria, VA
Copyright © 2025 R. M. Smith

All rights reserved including the right of reproduction
in whole or in part in any form.

Design and Layout by R. M. Smith

Summary: A high-contrast black and white baby book
featuring objects and pets around the house.

ISBN: 979-8999093806

First Edition
10 9 8 7 6 5 4 3 2 1

www.ingramcontent.com/pod-product-compliance
Lightning Source LLC
Chambersburg PA
CBHW052037030426
42337CB00027B/5041